# Oakland Baptist Church
## 1854 – 2004

150 Years of Faith and Faithfulness

Copyright © 2004 Edward DeVries
ISBN: 9798700807425

# Table of Contents

# Table of Contents – continued

Table of Contents – continued

# Introduction

A few weeks after my arrival as Pastor of the Oakland Baptist Church, while looking at the sign "established 1854," I realized that the church was approaching her 150th anniversary. At that moment the Holy Spirit impressed upon me to write the church's history in a book.

But there were many obstacles along the way.

All of the records and archives of the Creath-Brazos Association prior to 1985 had been lost to a fire. And all records and archives of the Union Baptist Association previous to 1977 had been lost to flooding that occurred as a result of Tropical Storm Alliance. What little survived the flood were destroyed in an arson fire in 1987. The history of Oakland and several other churches in a large area of Texas was lost to these tragedies.

The church's available records consisted of a few scribblings in a spiral notebook and old checkbook registers.

So I went to the County Chamber of Commerce, Library, Historical Commission, Newspaper, County Archives, etc. in search of anything about the church. Each place had a page or two of information but the overall history was far from revealed in these findings.

The Librarian and County Historian both asked if I had read Joseph Boulet's 4-Volume <u>History of the Baptist Churches in Grimes County</u>. They said that Boulet's work, written in 1936 and 1937, while he pastored the Baptist Church in Anderson, contained a chapter on Oakland Baptist. So of course I was interested in reading this history but was originally unable to find a copy. Thankfully, Boulet's original manuscript was found in the attic of the Anderson Baptist Church and a copy was made for my use.

Seems that even back in 1936 Boulet had the same problem I was having in trying to write a history of Oakland. He prefaced his two-page history by saying:

> The records of the church seem not to have been well taken care of, and all of the minutes prior to 1916 seem to have vanished.

Even so, Boulet's history proved to be a valuable resource.

To add tragedy to tragedy, the records which Boulet mentions (1916 to 1936) were lost in the Thanksgiving Day fire of 1938 that took the home of Mrs. R.H. Allen.

A new record book was started in December of 1938 and was found by Mrs. Frieda Floyd when she was cleaning out the closet in her spare room. This provided excellent records of the minutes of the congregational conferences held through 2000. The book also had statistical records for these years but statistics were poorly kept during many years and not recorded at all during others. So complete records of conversions, additions, transfers, baptisms, funerals, enrollments, attendance, etc. do not exist.

The Presbyterian Church in the neighboring town of Shiro had maintained a history of many of the churches in

Grimes County. So they had a file of information on Oakland through 1979.

The local columnist for the Navasota Examiner had a few items of interest and her mother, who had written the column for 40 years previous, had a few more items.

The Archives at Baylor University contained reports filed with the now defunct Grimes County Baptist Association. These archives also contained biographical information and pictures of some of the church's former pastors.

The 1872 book <u>Flowers and Fruits in the Wilderness</u> by Rev. Z. N. Morrell, though a history of the early years of Texas, contained various mentions of Oakland, Roan's Prairie, and biographical information about the church's early pastors. I am thankful that the Lord led me to this treasured book.

The longer-standing Baptist churches in Grimes County and the Baptist History Museum in neighboring Washington County were consulted, the older members of Oakland as well as the elder residents of the Roan's Prairie community were interviewed, former pastors were found and interviewed, etc.

Through these efforts, slowly but surely, the Lord enabled me to piece together the history of the Oakland Baptist Church. I was also privileged to make several friends in the process.

As I've discovered the history of Oakland Baptist Church I've gained a new appreciation for men such as George

Baines, James Stribling, and J.M. Carroll. I am honored to have had the privilege of sharing in their labor for a season.

It is my hope that this book will record and preserve for posterity the history of Oakland Baptist Church. And, more importantly, wherever this volume is read, that it will bring glory and honor to the Lord Jesus Christ, who is the Head of the Church.

Ed DeVries
John 3:30

Section 1:

# THE HISTORY
# OF THE
# OAKLAND BAPTIST CHURCH

# Chapter 1: 1854 – 1936

In 1854, while serving as pastor of the Anderson Baptist Church, George W. Baines began holding services one Sunday each month on the Three-Notch Road near the Kennard Cemetery some 7 or 8 miles northeast of Anderson. From these meetings the Lake Creek Baptist Church was organized on July 29th with 14 members reported.

In 1855 the young church began holding its services in a two-story frame structure located on Oakland Hill. Oakland Hill was a high point on the stage coach line and proved to be an excellent location for the new congregation. So when the location was selected by the church as its permanent meeting house the name of the church was changed from Lake Creek Baptist Church to Oakland Baptist Church.

In October of 1855 the church invited D.B. Morrill to preach a revival. The county newspaper for November 7, 1855 reported that the meeting resulted in 20 conversions, 21 baptisms, and 8 people joining the church by transfer of letter. At the revival's end, Reverend Morrill reported the church's membership to have grown to 56. Considering the time and size of the town this was a large membership.

In 1856 the church petitioned for inclusion in the Union Baptist Association. The petition was granted. In the church's initial report to the association the membership was stated to be 71.

In 1861 President Abraham Lincoln ordered the invasion of the Southern States and the War of Northern Aggression or the War for Southern Independence began. The war took its toll on the State of Texas and on the churches in the State. But Oakland continued to grow during the war. At the war's end, only three churches in Texas were able to support their pastor financially. Oakland was one of those three.

The Baptist General Convention Statistics for 1871 reported Oakland to have 100 members. This made it the largest Baptist church in Texas for that year. The church had outgrown the Oakland Hill meeting house and plans were made for the church to secure land and build a regular house of worship.

J. W. Mayfield donated $100 and a keg of nails. This started a building fund that would quickly raise $2,000. The lot of land between the old Oakland Hill meeting house and the Stage Coach Depot was purchased and the building was built (except for the ceiling) and dedicated in 1872. The ceiling was installed in the 1880's.

In 1898 the annual meeting of the Grimes County Baptist Association was held on September 21st and 22nd at Oakland's meeting house. Oakland's pastor, R.J. McGinty, was appointed to preach the opening sermon.

In 1913, under the direction of Pastor George N. Cook, the church decided to move the meeting house approximately one and a half miles from its location on Oakland Hill to its present location in Roan's Prairie. The church paid just $45 for the new plot of land. The meeting house was rolled on long logs and pulled by a team of oxen. This was a slow process that took the better part of the fall and winter months to complete.

The meeting house was fully restored in 2003 and the church still holds its weekly services in this beautiful building.

The church's annual reports demonstrate the membership to be in a constant state of fluctuation from 1875 – 1935:

1875: 132
1882: 30
1897: 89
1899: 97
1900: 96
1909: 115
1917: 128
1930: 35
1932: 50
1935: 30

Sunday School enrollment also varied during these years from anywhere between 12 and 86.

A newspaper article lists the following as the regular attendants of the church's services in 1905: Henry Cone family, Perry Taylor family, George Jolly family, Jim Taylor family, Robert H. Allen family, Bob Dreher family, Will McIntyre family, J.W. Cuthrell family, Jess Statham family, Anton Garvin family, J.W. Boher family, Rowland Newton family, Don Ratliff family, Will Shellman family, John Conner family, Maxie McIntyre family, Jesse Floyd family,

Charlie Floyd family, Allen Martin family, and Frank Hemler family.

The following are listed in <u>The History of the Baptist Churches of Grimes County</u> as having served as Sunday School Superintendent during the years up to and including 1936: William W. Walker, Calvin D. Uzzell, T.V. Williamson, H.S. Cone, J. W. Baker, J.O. Mc Intyre, W. Todd. Terrell, and Robert J. Dreher.

According to annual reports L.M. Ratliff, H.J. Gooch, A.R. Gooch, J.L. Gillespie, P.D. Taylor, J.W. Baker, Robert J. Dreher, C.C. Floyd, and W.L. Mc Intyre served as Clerks.

The known Deacons during this time frame were Sim T. Taylor, Calvin D. Uzzell, P. D. Taylor, H. S. Cone, M. J. Mc Intyre, J.W.Baker, Robert J. Dreher, C.C. Floyd, and W.L. Mc Intyre.

Several men served as pastor during these years. The most noteworthy were George W. Baines, D. B. Morrill, J.E. Paxton, Justin A. Kimball, James H. Stribling, and Dr. James Milton Carroll.

The founding pastor, George W. Baines, one of the 19th century's great church planters, established 3 churches in Arkansas and planted several more in Texas, including Oakland. He was the great-grandfather of the nation's 36th President, Lyndon Baines Johnson.

The second pastor, D.B. Morrill, was a renowned businessman from Galveston Island. He was also the first ministerial graduate of Baylor University. He served Oakland from 1856-1857.

J.E. Paxton was moderator of the Texas Baptist State Convention and chaired many of the convention's committees. He was the pastor from 1859–1860.

Dr. Justin A. Kimball was editor of the State Baptist newspaper. He served the church from 1862–1866.

James H. Stribling, reported to have been the most popular preacher in Texas in the 1860's and 70's, pastored Oakland in 1869.

From 1878 – 1879 Dr. James Milton Carroll, undisputedly the greatest Baptist historian of all time, pastored Oakland. Dr. Carroll wrote the famous Baptist History textbook <u>The Trail of Blood</u>.

Working together with the churches of the Union, Evergreen, Grimes County, Creath, and Creath-Brazos Baptist Associations and with the Texas Baptist State Convention and the Baptist General Convention of Texas; Oakland was always active in denominational affairs.

In 1919 the Baptist General Convention records that Oakland made a very sizable contribution to that year's 75 Million Campaign.

Preaching services during this period were originally held on the last Sunday of the month. At some unrecorded point in time this was changed and the meetings began to be held every 1$^{st}$ and 3$^{rd}$ Sunday.

# Chapter 2: 1937 – 1953

From 1937 to 1950 the church conducted Sunday School on a weekly basis and had preaching services on the 1st and 3rd Sundays of each month.

A fire at the home of Mrs. R.H. Allen on Thanksgiving Day, 1938 destroyed all of the church's records. A new minute and record book was started on December 4, 1938.

The Sunday School report for 1940 records an enrollment of 55 people.

In 1939 and 1940 Revivals were conducted by a Bro. Etheridge from Huntsville. The record book says these meetings resulted in "several additions." Bro. Etheridge conducted another revival in 1941 with no additions recorded.

The World War II years were especially difficult for the church. All of the young men were overseas fighting in the war and the older men and women were forced into mass migration to the cities so that they could find work. This population shift resulted in such a drastic reduction in the church's membership and attendance that Pastor W.H. Jones resigned in 1942 "leaving the little church for dead."

In August of 1943, even though the church was without a pastor, a revival was conducted by E.K. Shepherd who was then pastor of the Baptist Church in nearby Bedias. Two additions were recorded as a result of this meeting.

In 1945 Pastor Kelley of the Shiro Baptist Church drove to Roans Prairie on several Sunday afternoons to conduct preaching services in the Oakland meeting house. At some point during the year he conducted a week-long revival.

Another revival was conducted in July of 1946 by Pastor Hendricks of the Bedias Baptist Church. This meeting resulted in 1 conversion and 4 additions.

The church stirred in 1948 and called Harold Dickerson as pastor. He was then a student at the Southwestern Baptist Theological Seminary in Fort Worth. He did a marvelous work. A week-long revival was conducted in 1948 by missionary Lemuel Hall.

In March of 1948 the church purchased new hymnals and in April of the same year Mrs. E.A. Bode, Mrs. Erving Thomas, and Mrs. Jesse Floyd donated the chairs that still set on the platform behind the pulpit. It was also recorded that $88 was given to foreign missionaries during the year and the total monies spent by the church (including the pastor's salary) was $1,212.

In 1949 Pastor Dickerson donated the pulpit that at the time of this writing still graces the church's platform.

In July of 1949 the pastor of the Missionary Baptist Church in Navasota preached a week-long revival for Oakland. This meeting resulted in 3 recorded additions.

In 1950 Howard Parshall became the pastor. At this time the church voted to change its preaching services from the 1st and 3rd to the 2nd and 4th Sundays of each month.

Brother Parshall pastored Oakland until his graduation from seminary when he accepted the call to the Baptist church in Weimer.

From April 9th-23rd, 1950 an extended nightly revival meeting was held in the meeting house. Several men preached during the course of the meeting. The meeting resulted in 5 conversions and 5 baptisms.

An 8-day revival starting on June 3, 1951 was conducted by Evangelist Jimmie Jones of Richards, Texas. This meeting resulted in 2 recorded decisions.

Starting on August 2, 1953 Pastor Beasley of the Emmanuel Baptist Church in Bryan conducted a week-long revival. The church record book reported the nightly attendance as "good" and the sermons as "wonderful." 2 additions were recorded during the meeting.

On December 13, 1953 the church ordained Ralph Hogue to the Gospel Ministry. Rev. E.L. Moody, Director of Missions for the Creath-Brazos Association was chairman of the ordination council.

# Chapter 3: 1954 – 1979

This chapter will cover the years from the church's 100th Anniversary to her 125th Anniversary.

In 1954 the church celebrated its 100th Anniversary with a special service on July 29th. 150 people signed the guestbook on that day. It is safe to assume that the actual attendance was slightly higher because there were probably some folks who didn't sign the guestbook.

Vacation Bible School was held in 1954 with 54 children in attendance. The Sunday School report for that year recorded an average weekly attendance of 25.

Each year from 1958 through 1982 the church would sponsor an annual "homecoming" in September. It would be an all day event that started at 10 AM with Sunday School followed by the regular preaching service. Then there would be a dinner on the grounds, an afternoon program, and usually a "singing." Below is a record of the date of each homecoming for which the church has a guestbook followed by the number of people who signed the guestbook. Of course, the actual attendance on those days was most likely higher as it is certain that not all guests signed the book.

9-28-1958: 106
9-20-1959: 144
9-18-1960: 141
9-17-1961: 199
9-16-1962: 156

9-15-1963: 77
9-27-1964: 75
9-26-1965: 117
9-26-1968: 56
9-16-1979: 105

While large crowds were drawn to the annual homecomings and other special services, the attendance on a typical Sunday morning during these years fluctuated from between 4 to 20 people.

In 1964 the church reported the following teachers and officers:

Mr. L.B. Floyd – Sunday School Superintendent and Song Leader
Mr. J.S. Bracewell – Adult Teacher
Mrs. Frieda Floyd – Intermediate Teacher
Mrs. J.O. McIntyre – Treasurer
Mrs. T.J. Slayton – Pianist
Barbara McDougald – Clerk

Sister Joyce Floyd remembers Mrs. Slayton conducting annual Vacation Bible schools from 1959 through the mid-1960's.

In 1971 the church reported 8 active members. In 1972 the records indicated that 5 people joined the church raising the number to 13.


REVIVALS

The Church recorded six revival meetings during the years 1955-1974.

On July 31, 1955 a Rev. Bonner from Iola began a week-long revival meeting. In 1956 a revival was conducted by a Rev. Crouch of Navasota. On July 18, 1960 a Bro. Hardy held a meeting and in 1961 the revival was conducted by Jim Manley.

On June 6, 7, and 8th of 1969 Evangelist Jimmy Darnell preached a 3-night revival that drew crowds of over 100 people each night.

The church's last revival during this period was recorded to have been conducted from October 21st-25th, 1974.


## 125th ANNIVERSARY

On June 10, 1979 the church held a special service to commemorate its upcoming 125th Anniversary. The guestbook for that service had 67 signatures.


## MEETING HOUSE IMPROVEMENTS

In 1954 the wood burning stoves were replaced with a gas heating system at a cost of $350.

In 1961 the church underwent two major renovations. The first was the result of a February decision to wire the church for electricity. The second major improvement came in May of 1961 when the church voted to build a cinderblock building in the rear of the main building. This building featured two fully plumbed "modern" restrooms.

At some time between 1962 and 1968 a wall was built that divided the church's building into two rooms. The front two-thirds of the building remained the building's main auditorium and worship area and the back third was converted into a kitchen and fellowship hall. For a brief time in 1968 a portion of the rear room was sectioned off for use as a bedroom and temporary parsonage.

In 1966 the State of Texas declared the church's building to be a historical landmark and added the structure to the state's Register of Historical Places – a certificate was signed by the Governor and presented to the church. In 1967 a historical marker plaque was installed on the northeast corner of the meeting house.

In 1969 the church purchased a new piano for $450.

During this 25-year period preaching services were held on the 2$^{nd}$ and 4$^{th}$ Sundays of each month. 10 different men (listed in chapter 9) served as pastor. Tommy McDougald (1959–1965) and Neal Todd (1973–1979) being the two with the longest terms of service at six years each.

Pastor McDougald is now retired and living in nearby Iola. He tells me that he and many of the other pastors at Oakland during these years were seminary students who would drive down from Fort Worth on Sundays. During the years he served at Oakland he also pastored a church in Wheelock on the 2 Sundays of each month that Oakland did not have services. He says that some of the other pastors also held a second pastorate in addition to their ministry at Oakland.

The church continued to hold its annual "homecomings" in 1980, 81, and 82. Below is the recorded number of people who signed the guestbook for each homecoming:

9-21-1980: 84
9-20-1981: 76
9-19-1982: 132

The typical Sunday morning attendance during the years 1980-1985 was 5 or 6 people.

In 1986 the church called Bob Brock as their pastor. Oakland was his first pastorate. It was under his ministry that the church began meeting for services on a weekly basis. An article in the July 23, 1986 Creath-Brazos Association newsletter credits Pastor Brock with having revived the church. The article states that as a result of his outreach efforts the church grew to an average attendance in the upper 20's. Mention is also made of 10 youth from the church attending an outing at Washington on the Brazos State Park.

Pastor Brock preached his last sermon at Oakland on August 9, 1987. Mrs. Frieda Floyd wrote the following in the church record book on that day:

> Rev. Bob Brock preached his last sermon...every member cried. It is a sad day for us all...he was a wonderful pastor.

When Pastor Brock resigned the church's attendance immediately dropped to just 8 people. A Retired pastor from Bryan, Texas, Brother McBeth, filled the pulpit for the next few weeks as the remaining members moved their letters to other churches. This left only Bernard and Frieda Floyd as members of the church.

On Wednesday, September 2, 1987 Brother McBeth preached the "last" service. He had told the Floyds that he would continue to come and preach on Sundays but the Floyds, as the only two remaining members, voted unanimously to stop holding services.

The Floyds began attending the services of other churches in the county but they maintained their membership in the Oakland Church with hopes that they could resume services at a future date.

In March of 1988 Mrs. Frieda Floyd made an entry in the record book that the church was still not holding any type of regular services but that her family and some other former members were holding a fundraiser to make some needed repairs to the building.

The fundraiser was a success. Several thousand dollars were raised resulting in the building being leveled, the understructure of the building being reinforced, all of the windows being replaced, a new roof installed, the siding reworked, the building painted, and several other needful repairs were completed.

In 1989 Kenneth and Evelyn Gilbert met with the Floyds and expressed an interest in joining the church. On May 7,

1989 the Floyd and Gilbert families re-instituted the Sunday School with 10 children in attendance. The following week there were 9, the week after that 12. In October Brother Larry Anderson of Hilltop Baptist Church began coming on Sunday afternoons to conduct preaching services.

In April of 1990 Brother Anderson was replaced by Stephen Jeffries, pastor of the Baptist Church in Navasota. Bro. Jeffries did not accept the pastorate of Oakland, but like Brother Anderson, he came on Sunday afternoons and conducted weekly preaching services.

In the fall of 1991 Wes Miller, a student at nearby Texas A&M University, accepted the call to serve as pastor. He served until his graduation in the spring of 1992.

During the period from 1992 until 1994 Mrs. Frieda Floyd and Brother Kenneth Gilbert would conduct Sunday School in the morning and pastors from the Baptist churches in Huntsville or Shiro would come in the afternoon and conduct preaching services. The church had no official pastor during the period.

The weekly preaching and Sunday School attendance fluctuated from 9 to 15 during the years 1989 to 1996.

In 1994 Judge James Dixon joined the church. He began teaching the adult Sunday School class. While he was not an ordained minister he performed the duties of the pastor from 1995 through October of 2003. He was faithful to teach, preach, and visit during these years.

The weekly attendance during the years 1996 to 2003 fluctuated from 3 to 21 people. The church's average weekly attendance for the year 2002 was 4.

 A special candlelight service was held on December 2, 2000. The church guestbook was signed by 31 people on that day.

# Chapter 5: 2003 – 2004

Having been built in 1872, by 2003, 131 years were beginning to take their toll on the meeting house. A gift given in the will of Mrs. Jessie Mae Bode of Roan's Prairie provided the necessary funds to make the repairs. Robert Smith of nearby Richards was contracted to do the work.

On September 23rd I was attending a meeting at the Grimes County Courthouse in Anderson. Afterward, while talking in the parking lot to a retired Pastor, Dan Bates of Millican, I made the following comment:

> I would give up my whole evangelistic itinerary if I could just find a church within a reasonable driving distance that had 20 or 30 folks meeting in an old white frame building that was built back in the 1800's.

Contractor Robert Smith overheard the comment and gave me the telephone number of Brother Ronnie Floyd. On October 19th I preached with 3 of the church's 4 members and 4 visitors in attendance.

On November 2nd I accepted the church's call to serve as Pastor. It was then determined by the church that I would receive an offering of $30 each week. In addition to serving at Oakland, I would continue to serve as the President of the School of Biblical & Theological Studies, and as Chaplain of the Sons of Confederate Veterans.

On Sunday November 9th I announced a bold program that would enable the church to present the gospel to every home in Grimes County by the end of 2004. This program would include mass mailings, aggressive door-to-door campaigns, video evangelism, establishing a church website, special events, and a revival. The membership's response was extremely enthusiastic.

Secretary Joyce Floyd pledged the money for the first mass-mailing campaign and she and I together pledged the money to produce several hundred copies of a powerful 17-minute video titled "Somewhere Forever."

Through mail and door-to-door efforts these gospel preaching videos were placed in homes throughout Grimes County.

The week of November 10th several hours were devoted to the development of a multi-page internet website detailing the church's ministries. We announced the launch of the website on November 19th.

The month of December was spent meeting the town's business people, ranchers, and prominent citizens. Also, during this time I traveled throughout Grimes County and nearby Madisonville and College Station to call on various county officials, the editors of the various area newspapers, and the Postmasters of the area's Post Offices. The month was spent becoming familiar with and praying over the area.

The church ordained William "Bill" Sandoval to the Gospel Ministry on December 21st. Bill was a mid-year graduate of the School of Biblical & Theological Studies. He and his wife Patti have started a church in East Moline, Illinois.

After holding a few services in a hotel conference room they were given a beautiful parsonage and brick meeting house formerly belonging to a Plymouth Brethren congregation. It was my privilege to preach the dedication service for the building.

## 2004 RENOVATION OF RESTROOMS

On one of my first Sunday's at Oakland I went to the rear of the meeting house to use the restroom facility. Upon opening the door I was greeted by a 5 foot rattle-snake. Fortunately it was a cold day and the creature had wrapped himself around a ceiling joist and wasn't in a position to strike. Mrs. Floyd told me that it had probably been at least 5 years since anyone had used the facilities and she didn't even think they worked. After a plumbing inspection it was determined that the septic line had collapsed. In January a plumber was contracted to repair the septic line and Brother Ronnie Floyd cleaned and otherwise reworked the bathrooms so that they would once again be functional and attractive.

## RADIO INTERVIEW

On January 14th I was interviewed by Navasota News Radio (1550 AM). This was a great opportunity to witness for Christ and familiarize the residents of the county with the ministries of the church. Two visitors attended as a result of the radio interview.

# ROBERT E. LEE SUNDAY

On January 18, 2004 the church hosted the first in its series of planned special services or "big days." In honor of Confederate Hero's Day and General Robert E. Lee's birthday the church hosted a Robert E. Lee Sunday.

Several ladies dressed in period hoop-dresses and I dressed as a Confederate Chaplain. The morning's music consisted of the General's favorite hymns and the title of the message was "The Christian Testimony of Robert E. Lee." Lee's life and faith were used as a foundation for preaching a clear gospel message. Special music was provided by Dan and Linda Bates of Millican.

After the service War Between the States re-enactors from the 12th Texas Cavalry and 11th Texas Infantry did a demonstration on the church lawn. Randy Billingsly of Maysfield donated the use of his canon for the event.

Mr. Gene Hightower, a Great-Great Grandson of General Lee was in attendance. He presented the church with a picture of the General reading the Bible to a small child. The picture was ceremoniously hung in the meeting house behind the Sunday School stand.

This special service recorded a total attendance of 84 with 74 first-time visitors. Several visitors professed faith during the invitation.

# REVIVAL

The one-day revival, with Dr. Roy Branson, president of Landmark Baptist University in Bristol, Tennessee, was held on February 8th. Special music was provided by Dan and Linda Bates. There were 10 visitors. Dr. Branson preached a message titled "The Triumphant Christ." Afterward, he gave an invitation during which every visitor made a profession of faith.

# FIRST PARKING LOT

Because of heavy rains during the days leading up to the Robert E. Lee Sunday there were three cars stuck in the field beside the meeting house during that event. Seeing a need and desiring to fill it, Randy Billingsly of Maysfield offered to donate his labor and the use of his dump truck and other paving equipment for the construction of a parking lot.

In February and March there were several weeks of horrible rains that continued to soak the ground around the meeting house. Something had to be done.

In mid-March Randy and I secured paving materials from the Grimes County Road and Bridge Department and on March 22-23rd Randy and his crew went to work. He re-enforced the circular driveway in front of the church and laid a parking lot with 12 parking spaces on the north side of the meeting house.

# RESURRECTION DAY CELEBRATION

The third in the church's series of special services or "big days" was an Easter Sunday Celebration. An open letter to the community and church brochure was sent out in a mass-mailing to every home in Roans Prairie, Anderson, and Shiro in early April inviting the un-churched to a special Easter Sunday service.

The sermon text was taken from I Corinthians 15:3-8. Special music was provided by Dan and Linda Bates.

Everyone who attended the service received a complimentary copy of the book <u>Its Easter and I'm Excited</u> by Dr. Shelton Smith.

APRIL 25th

When preaching the week before Easter I had shared with the people the importance of determining the Lord's will for our lives and doing it. In the course of the message I encouraged the people, whenever they found themselves in a new place or situation, to pray and ask the Lord why He put them there and what they could do in that place or station to serve Him.

Of course, in the preparation of the message I found myself drawn to my knees and asking the Lord that very question.

> Lord, why have you put me in this place?
> What exactly is to be my ministry here?

The answer was disturbing. I felt as though the Holy Spirit was telling me that he had brought me to Oakland to research, rediscover, and record the church's history. It was as though the Lord was telling me that when that task was done He would be moving me.

While I shared with the congregation that I felt the Lord had placed me at Oakland to research and write the history, I chose to dismiss the part about my moving on afterward.

Well, without going into details, just a few days later, I had finished all but the final draft of this book. Once I had, the Lord providentially effected a series of events that, added together, made it very clear that it was time for me to move into a new ministry.

My message on the 25th was the culmination of a 4part series that began on the first Sunday of April with a message on The Crucifixion of Our Lord and ended that Sunday with The Soon Return of our Lord. Everyone attending the service on the 25th received a free copy of my 9-chapter book <u>Bible Teaching About the Rapture</u>.

After the close of the invitation, with great sorrow, I read the following letter of resignation to the congregation:

4-25-2004

Dear Members of Oakland Baptist Church,

It has been my privilege to serve as your pastor for the last 6 months. I will always be thankful to the Lord for the opportunity to have occupied the pulpit that was formerly home to many of my heros of the faith from a bygone era. Men who were key figures in the early life of Texas and of

19th century Baptist life. Men such as George Baines, J.M. Carroll, D.B. Morrill, B.H. Carroll, and Z.N. Morrell.

It is with great sadness that I tender resignation this morning.

I hope and pray that in my short time here I have, in some manner, been used of the Lord to be a blessing and encouragement in each of your lives.

I believe that the primary accomplishment of my ministry here at Oakland has been to research, and in most cases discover, the details of the church's 150-year history and record the same. The book, when published, will be about 120 pages. It is my intention to continue with the publication of this work for the benefit of the church and future generations.

If the church is without a pastor on August 1$^{st}$ I will gladly come on that day to moderate the 150$^{th}$ Anniversary Celebration activities and deliver the memorial message. I have already done much of the leg work for this event and would be happy to see these preparations to completion and serve the Church one last time in that capacity.  I would also consider it a privilege to participate in the events of that day because I do feel that I have had a part, however small, in the church's 150-year history.

Otherwise, I will stand behind the church's pulpit for the last time on May 7$^{th}$.

After the service this morning I will be turning over all church records and other information that will assist in the maintenance of the church's web-site and other ministries to our Church Secretary, Mrs. Joyce Floyd.

As always,

Wishing You All of God's Best!!
Pastor Ed DeVries
John 3:30

Afterward I talked with the folks as we all fellowshipped after the service and then I began preparing the building for the upcoming Southern Minister's Conference.


## SOUTHERN MINISTER'S CONFERENCE

On May 7th Oakland's meeting house hosted the first-annual meeting of the Texas Southern Heritage Minister's Conference. The meeting was a first of its kind gathering of Texas pastors and evangelical ministers who are members of and chaplains in the Sons of Confederate Veterans, United Daughters of the Confederacy, Order of the Confederate Rose, League of the South, Military Order of the Stars and Bars, and other Southern history/heritage groups.

Speakers for the day included Dr. John Weaver, a Georgia Pastor and Chaplain-in-Chief of the Sons of Confederate Veterans; Rev. Gillis Bartles; Pastor Don Majors, MOS&B Chaplain; Rev. Dan Bray; and myself. It was my privilege to moderate the meeting.

The building was filled to capacity with preachers from all across the State. The messages were excellent and we enjoyed a full breakfast and a grilled steak lunch. I was elected moderator for next year's meeting which will be held on May 6, 2005 in Hawkins, Texas.

So ended my season as the Pastor of the Oakland Baptist Church.

# 150th ANNIVERSARY CELEBRATION

The 150th Anniversary Celebration is scheduled for Sunday August 1, 2004. Since this book will go to press before then I must write of the service before it takes place. Because of this, I can not say with certainty exactly what will transpire on that day but I do know that several things are planned. There is a strong sense in which the celebration will be the culmination of the church's 150-year history. Therefore, it is only appropriate that this history of the church's first 150 years record something of the event.

The day will begin at 10 AM with a special commemorative service. Former pastors Sam Douglass, Tommy McDougald, and the widow of the late Pastor Gordon Graham will be the church's guests for this special Sunday. The day's events will also be attended by scores of Oakland's former members and attenders and by a number of former Roans Prairie residents.

After this service there will be a catered lunch in the Roans Prairie Community Center (across the street from the church's meeting house). This lunch will be followed by a special service at the Community Center. This luncheon service will have a cake with 150 candles followed by testimonies from former pastors and members.

Also during this time various letters congratulating the church on its 150 years of service will be read. Among them will be a Proclamation by the Commissioners of Grimes County recognizing July 29th as Oakland Baptist Church Day. I presented the necessary petition to the Commissioner's Court in March and the 5 members of the

Court voted unanimously to issue the Proclamation. The Proclamation reads as follows:

Grimes County, Texas

# Proclomation

Resolution acknowledging the spiritual leadership and dedication provided by the Oakland Baptist Church and for its numerous contributions to the people of the town of Roan's Prairie and to the people of Grimes County on occasion of its sesquicentennial anniversary of service.

**WHEREAS,** Oakland Baptist Church has served the people of the town of Roan's Prairie and the County of Grimes for 150 years; and,

**WHEREAS,** Oakland Baptist Church is the oldest Church in Roan's Prairie and one of the earliest churches of any denomination established in Grimes County; and,

**WHEREAS,** Oakland Baptist Church has continuously served its community in faith, religious proclamation, education, social service, and cultural enrichment; now, therefore, be it

**RESOLVED,** that the County of Grimes wishes to honor the work of the Oakland Baptist Church on its 150th anniversary of service, and, be it

**FURTHER RESOLVED,** that the Grimes County Court of Commissioners honors Oakland Baptist Church this 29th day of July 2004 and thanks the church for creating a better quality of life for its congregation and the community of Roan's Prairie, Grimes County, Texas.

After the luncheon everyone will meet in the yard beside the meeting house and take turns ringing the meeting house bell 150 times in honor of the 150<sup>th</sup> anniversary. Then everyone will return to the meeting house for an old-fashioned hymn-singing.

# Chapter 6:
## Oakland Baptist Church Cemetery

In 1867 the church sectioned off the back side of Oakland Hill for use as a cemetery. In 1872, when the church's present meeting house was built, it was built directly in front of the cemetery.

Today, the cemetery is known as the Old Oakland Cemetery and it is no longer owned or maintained by the Church. The Old Oakland Cemetery Association now owns the cemetery and Chairwoman Frieda Floyd oversees its maintenance and daily operation.

Several former members of the church are interred within its fence and a State of Texas historical marker at the main gate marks the cemetery as being the burial place of several early Texas pioneers.

As Chaplain for the Sons of Confederate Veterans, it was my privilege to decorate the graves of the following veterans of the Confederate States Army buried in the cemetery:

S. Bookman – ?/?/? to 4/14/1866
Harvey Brigance – 10/20/1820 to ?/?/1886
Rev. S.H. Buchanan – 9/2/1815 to 6/12/1898
R. Clements – 1/7/1814 to 11/30/1908
R.B. Clifton – 1/23/1843 to 11/30/1908
Henry Shrock Cone – ?/?/1848 to 12/8/1930
James V. Floyd – 10/9/1837 to 7/19/1913
Archibald Garvin – 11/13/1840 to 7/21/1909

S.M. Garvin – 4/20/1811 to 11/26/1861
John L. Gillespie – 9/25/1841 to 11/24/1906
W.E.J. Grissett – unknown
J.P.G. Harmon – 1/12/1839 to 1/1/1917
John A. Horton – 5/7/1822 to 6/16/1899
Marcus L. Kennard – 9/24/1821 to 4/24/1897
John Loggins – ?/?/1821 to 10/14/1908
A.R. Martin – unknown
J.R. McIntyre – unknown
Jessie C. McIntyre – 3-3-1835 to 6/13/1908
Isaac Nowell – unknown
Alexander C. Parker – 8/14/1835 to 2/9/1921
J.L. Peteete – 3/22/184/ to 8/24/1906
Sidney R. Peteete – 12/12/1837 to 5/2/1872
B.F. Ratliff – 4/28/1838 to 5/6/1906
Otis D. Shelman – 10/24/1822 to 1/22/1900
Perry D. Taylor – ?/?/1845 to ?/?/1918

In March of 2004 I ordered military headstones from the Veterans Administration for each of the above named Confederate Veterans.

Once these headstones are installed I will return to the cemetery to conduct a full military memorial service, complete with military honor guard, in honor of these men. As part of the memorial the name of each veteran will be called out and each will receive a 21-musket and canon-fire salute.

# Chapter 7: Funerals

The church's record book records the following funerals conducted between 1941 and 1995:

Spurgeon Murry – 1941
J.V. Floyd – 19??
Roland Nowlin – 1943
Charley Floyd – 1944
Jesse Floyd – 1944
Mrs. Clarence Floyd – 1945
Mrs. Mattie Hadey – 1947
Mr. N. L. Danford – 1947
Frank Helmer – 1949
Galvin Black – 1951
Mrs. Susie Bess – 1952
Mrs. R. J. Dreher – 1954
Richard Davidson – 1954
Mrs. Dean Stathan – 1954
Mrs. Fannie Allen – 1957
Mrs. Katie Hamilton – 1957
Willie McIntyre – 1957
Luther Danford – 1958
Mrs. Charlie Floyd – 1959
Mr. Lewis Floyd – 1971
Mrs. Roland Nowlin – 1972
Mrs. Jesse Floyd – 1978
Mrs. Bessie Floyd – 3/14/1979
Mr. Dean Stathan – 1979
Mr. Orion McIntyre – 1984
Mrs. Bettie Statham – 1984
Mrs. Bracewell – 8/5/1985

Mrs. Delitha McIntyre – 1986
Bernard Floyd – 1991
Evelyn Gilbert 5/22/1995
Wanda Brandt Peteete (after 1995)

# Chapter 8: Baptisms

Naturally one of the first questions that a new pastor asks when the meeting house does not have a baptistery is "where do we baptize folks?"

Oakland Baptist Church has baptized people in the baptistery of the Shiro Baptist Church for as long as any of the current members can remember (since the 1950's). But the church at Shiro was organized several years after the Oakland Church so where did the church baptize before the 1950's?

Mrs. Doris Thomas, a 93-year-old life-long resident of Roan's Prairie, who is now confined to a nursing home facility in nearby College Station, remembers the church baptizing in a man-made pond that was dug out near the meeting house's current location. She says that when she was a girl the land around the church was a cattle ranch and there was a small man-made pond that was dug out about 250 yards from the meeting house. Rainwater kept it full and it was the watering hole for the cows. As a girl on that ranch she says she remembers watching as several people were baptized in the cow pond.

In the 1950's the old pond was filled in with dirt but the approximate size and shape of the area can be surmised because the ground in that area is sunken about 2-6 inches lower than the surrounding ground.

The church most likely used the cow pond as its Baptizing Hole for most of the time from 1914 – 1950.

As to where the church baptized from 1854–1913, well that is anybody's guess since no location is recorded.

Standing at the cemetery, the location of the church's second meeting house (1855-1872) and of its third (1872-1913), one can see a drop off and a tree line amidst a cow pasture about 600 yards off in the distance. Walking over there you'll discover the beginning of a creek that, if followed for several miles, will bring you to the Navasota River.

At the time I made this discovery the area had just finished about 3 weeks of daily steady down-pouring rains. I had to walk well over a mile before the water in the creek was deep enough to submerge someone. Under ordinary conditions the creek at this location would have been nearly dry. Of course, in the 1800's the water level of the creek could have been totally different.

While there is no way to know for sure, my educated guess is that during the years when the church met on Oakland Hill it either baptized its converts in some spot along the creek or in the Navasota River.

RECORDED BAPTISMS

Statistical tables for the Grimes County Baptist Association indicate that 33 people were baptized by Oakland Baptist Church during the four year period from 1987 to 1900.

1897: 12 baptisms
1898: 12 baptisms
1899: 4 baptisms

1900: 5 baptisms

The following 21 baptisms were recorded in the church record book during the years 1939-1972:

Jimmie McIntyre – 1939
Mrs. Roy Jordan – 1939
Maurice Jordan – 1939
Junior McIntyre – 1939
Jesse Statum, Jr. – 1939
Mrs. August Colby – 1943
Laurence Colby – 1943
Dorris Boyd – 1944
Ella May Statum – 1944
Mary Joe Statum – 1944
August Colby – 1946
George Floyd – 1948
D. C. Bullard – 1950
Gary Bullard – 1950
Mrs. Maurice Jordan – 1954
Earl Statum – 1954
Joyce Floyd – 1959
Ronnie Floyd – 1959
Norman Wayne Lewis – 1968
Norman Wayne – Jan. 12, 1969
Robin Gay – April 15, 1972

# Chapter 9:
# Pastors of Oakland Baptist Church

The following is a listing of the 47 men who have served as Pastor of the Oakland Baptist Church. Each pastor's dates of service are listed below his name.

George W. Baines
1854-1855

D.B. Morrill
1856-1857

J.E. Paxton
1859-1860

Dr. Justin A. Kimball
1862-1866

George W. Green
1868, 1870-1876, 1880

James H. Stribling
1869

J.A. Hill
1877

Dr. James Milton Carroll
1878-1879

G.H.M. Wilson
1881

George N. Cook
1886 and 1912-1913

G.M. Daniel
1887-1894

J.N. Clayton
1895-1896

R.J. McGinty
1897-1905

Joseph E. Boulet
1906-1908

J.M. Parker
1909-1910

T.M. West
1911

W. Finch
1914

W.H. Jones
1916-1920

D.L. McDowell
1921

J.F. High
1922

T.J. Touchberry
1924

J.G. Brock
1925

W.N. Purcell
1927

G.F. Purvis
1930

Basil Halbert
1932

G. E. Stewart
1935

W.H. Jones
1937-1942

Harold Dickerson
1948-1949

George Williams
1950-1951

Howard Parshall
1951-1952

Ralph Hogue
1953-1955

Glenn Brown
1955-1956

Ken Bradberry
1957-1958

T.B. Prescott
1958-1959

Thomas McDougald
1959-1965

Gordon Graham
1965-1968

Bill Darnell
1968-1970

Ken Howard
1970-1971

Sam Douglas
1972

Neal Todd
1973-1979

Frank Purvis
1979-1980

Jerry Crocker
1981-1982

Jack W. Mitchell
1984-1985

Bob Brock
1986-1987

Wes Miller
1991-1992

Hon. James Paul Dixon
Interim Pastor
1994-2003

Dr. Edward R. DeVries
2003-2004

# Chapter 10:
# Famous Texans Associated
# with Oakland Baptist Church

As was previously stated, all of Oakland's records prior to 1938 were lost in a fire. The reports and records filed with the Union Baptist Association are likewise unavailable because they too were lost in a flood and subsequent fire.

So much of the church's history from the period 1854-1938 will never be recovered. It is lost forever. We'll never know on this side of heaven the names of those who were converted, baptized, or transformed as a result of the church's ministry during this time period. Likewise, we'll never know the names of all of the many folks who visited, attended, were members, etc.

But it is established that at least 3 famous Texans enjoyed a strong association with the church between the years 1855-1879.

## SAM HOUSTON

Before coming to Texas, Sam Houston had served as Governor of Tennessee. During the years 1836-1861 Houston served as Commanding General of the Army that won the Texas War for Independence, President of the Republic of Texas, Governor of the State of Texas, and as a United States Senator from Texas.

During the years from 1855 until Houston's death in 1863 the church's meeting houses were immediately next to the depot for the stagecoach line that traveled from the capitol to Huntsville. The stagecoach passed by the church's meeting house on an almost daily basis and the stage always stopped at the depot. This made Sam Houston a regular traveler to the area, bringing him into regular contact with most of the church's members.

Houston, a member of the Baptist Church in Independence, was also a regular attendee of the meetings held at various churches throughout Grimes County and the Brazos Valley.

Given Sam Houston's religious activity and the fact that he would have traveled to the depot next to the meeting house on a weekly basis it is very likely that at some point he attended the church's services.

Considering that the 1855 revival conducted by D.B. Morrill was the biggest in the State up to that date, and given the fact that Morrill was a fellow member with Houston of the Independence Baptist Church, it is very likely that Sam Houston attended at least some of the services during this meeting.

Houston was also known to have given thousands of dollars toward the planting of new Baptist churches and towards the support of other Baptist works. In 1858 Houston established a joint stock company to finance the Texas Baptist Publication Society and the state's Baptist newspaper, The Texas Baptist.

Dr. Justin A. Kimball assumed the editorship of The Texas Baptist in 1861 when George Baines resigned his ownership of the newspaper to assume the presidency of Baylor College. In 1862 Dr. Kimball accepted the pastorate at Oakland and from 1862-1866 The Texas Baptist was published as a ministry of the Oakland Baptist Church.

During the years 1862-1865 a nation-wide paper shortage, due in large part to the War of Northern Aggression, was forcing religious newspapers across the Southland to cease publication. Sam Houston, not wanting to see The Texas Baptist suffer the fate of other newspapers, gave a considerable contribution to the church so that Pastor Kimball could buy paper and continue printing the newspaper. This proved to be a short-lived extension of the paper's life because as the war drug on the price of paper kept going up until ultimately, despite the best efforts of Houston and Kimball, The Texas Baptist, along with many other newspapers in the State, was forced to stop printing until after the war.

## Z.N. MORRELL

Arriving in 1835, Z.N. Morrell was the second Baptist preacher to arrive in the territory now known as Texas. He organized several churches in the "pioneer" days and served as Chaplain-in-Chief to the Army of the Republic during Texas' bid for independence from Mexico. He was an advisor to Sam Houston (both in Tennessee and Texas), the organizer of the first Baptist association in Texas, and moderator of the first Baptist Convention organized in the State.

Morrell did not pastor Oakland. But he did make several references to the church and to her various early pastors in his book <u>Flowers and Fruits in the Wilderness</u>, an accounting of his ministerial activity in Texas from 1835 through the 1870's. This indicates that Morrell maintained an ongoing relationship with the church from the time of its organization until the time of his death.

Given the vigorous itinerant preaching schedule that he maintained during this period it is very likely that he preached at Oakland on at least a few occasions.

He makes mention of the revival preached by D.B. Morrill in 1855 and provides the details of the meeting. While he may have given these reports second-hand, at that time in his life he usually did not write of events that he was not personally involved in.

I have no doubt that much of the church's early success was in response to the prayers of this great pioneer preacher.


## B.H. CARROLL

Dr. B.H. Carroll was the primary professor of theological subjects at Baylor University from 1872-1905. Later, with the help of Dr. J. Frank Norris, he established Southwestern Baptist Theological Seminary in Fort Worth where he served as the school's first President. In the latter part of the 19th century and at the beginning of the 20th he was the premier leader of Baptists in Texas. He was a first-rate scholar, able teacher and preacher, author, expositor, soul-winner, and contender for the faith.

Several of Carroll's students pastored Oakland during their college days. From 1878-1879 his brother, James Milton Carroll, served as Oakland's pastor. Because of this, Oakland was a blessed recipient of the preaching and teaching ministry of Dr. B.H. Carroll on several occasions.

# Chapter 11: Miscellaneous

## AFFILIATION AFTER 1987

In 1987, when Bernard Floyd notified the Creath-Brazos Association that Oakland would no longer be holding services, the association dropped the church from its membership list. In subsequent years the Baptist General Convention of Texas and the Southern Baptist Convention also dropped Oakland from their roles due to inactivity and the fact that they were not receiving annual reports or offerings from the church.

Oakland did not make any efforts to renew its association with any of the above named agencies. Hence, Oakland has been an Independent Baptist Church since 1989.

In March of 2004 the church received an invitation to renew its membership in the Creath-Brazos Association and with the Southern Baptist Convention. The church decided not to accept the invitation, choosing not to pursue formal relations with any denominational bodies.

## OAKLAND BAPTIST CHURCH SCHOOL

The building that the church used for a meeting house in the 1850's-60's was also used as a school house. If the school was a ministry of the church or just happened to meet in the same building is unclear.

The "old-timers" in the area remember stories of their parents attending school in the church's present meeting house and some even attended there themselves. They called it the Oakland Baptist Church School. Nobody seems to know if the school was so called because it was a ministry of the church, or if it was called by that name simply because it met in the church's building and was taught by ladies who also happened to be members of the church.

## OAKLAND "METHODIST CHURCH"

At different times in the history of Roan's Prairie the Methodists attempted to establish a church in the town. At one point they had a meeting house of their own but sold it.

At various times through the years, when the Methodists wanted to have services in Roan's Prairie, they would schedule them for the two Sundays a month opposite of when Oakland was having preaching so they could lease the Oakland meeting house on those Sundays.

The area "old timers" and the Floyds remember the Methodists holding their services in Oakland's meeting house but there are no records of the years when these services were held or the amount paid for use of the building.

# MEETING HOUSE DOORS

The custom in the middle 19th century was to build a meeting house with two full sets of doors. The men would enter through one side and the ladies on the other. The Oakland meeting house was built by this design as is shown in the 19th century photograph of the church in Section 2.

At some point in time in the 20th century the two doors were boarded up and a new double doorway was cut in the middle of the building.

When sitting in the meeting house and looking to either side of the main entryway the location of the two old doors is plainly indicated by the variation in the board pattern.


# PEWS

An undated letter written by Mrs. Frieda Floyd which is in the church's records mentions that the pews that are presently in the church's auditorium are the old pews from the Shiro Presbyterian Church. The date that these pews were donated is not recorded.

The church's record book shows that in October of 1996 $1,680 was spent to have these pews reconstructed.

Today the church only has 2 of its "original" pews. They are lined up against the two long walls in the fellowship hall.

# PICNIC TABLES

Mrs. Mignon Slayton recalls the wooded area in front of the church having several picnic tables during the decades of the 1950's and 1960's and that during those years it was very common for the church's members to have fellowship meals on the grounds after the morning services. It was also a popular place for area residents to have weekday afternoon picnics. She does not remember when the tables were removed.

# PULPIT-TOTING PREACHER

I have been told stories about a man who is simply referred to as the "pulpit-toting preacher." He is called by that name because nobody can remember his proper name but they do remember that he always brought a pulpit with him when he came to preach on Sundays.

He was not a pastor of the church but served as a supply minister at times when the church was without a pastor.

The years in which he supplied is not recalled but I would guess, given the folks who tell the stories, that it was during the 1960's or 70's.

What everyone does recall is that he was a retired pastor, was very eccentric, and he didn't like the church's pulpit. So he brought his own with him every Sunday. He'd arrive early, set up his pulpit, and when he was finished preaching he'd load it back up and take it home with him.

Section 2:

# PHOTO ALBUM
# OF THE
# OAKLAND BAPTIST CHURCH

# Photographs of the Meeting House
## Photo's taken in March of 2004

Meeting House – Built in 1872

Sign in front of the
Meeting House

Old Bell beside
the Meeting House

# Photographs of the Meeting House
Photo's taken in December of 2003

Inside the Meeting House

Pulpit and Platform

# Photographs of the Meeting House
## Photo's taken in March of 2004

Fellowship Hall

Outbuilding with "Modern Facilities"

# Old Pictures of the Meeting House

This picture, taken in the late 19th Century, was found in the Texas Baptist Historical Collection Archives

1960's oil painting by Mrs. Mignon Slayton

# The Old Oakland Cemetery
Photo's taken in March of 2004

Cemetery Entrance and Gate

Pioneer Graves

Historical Marker on the Meeting House

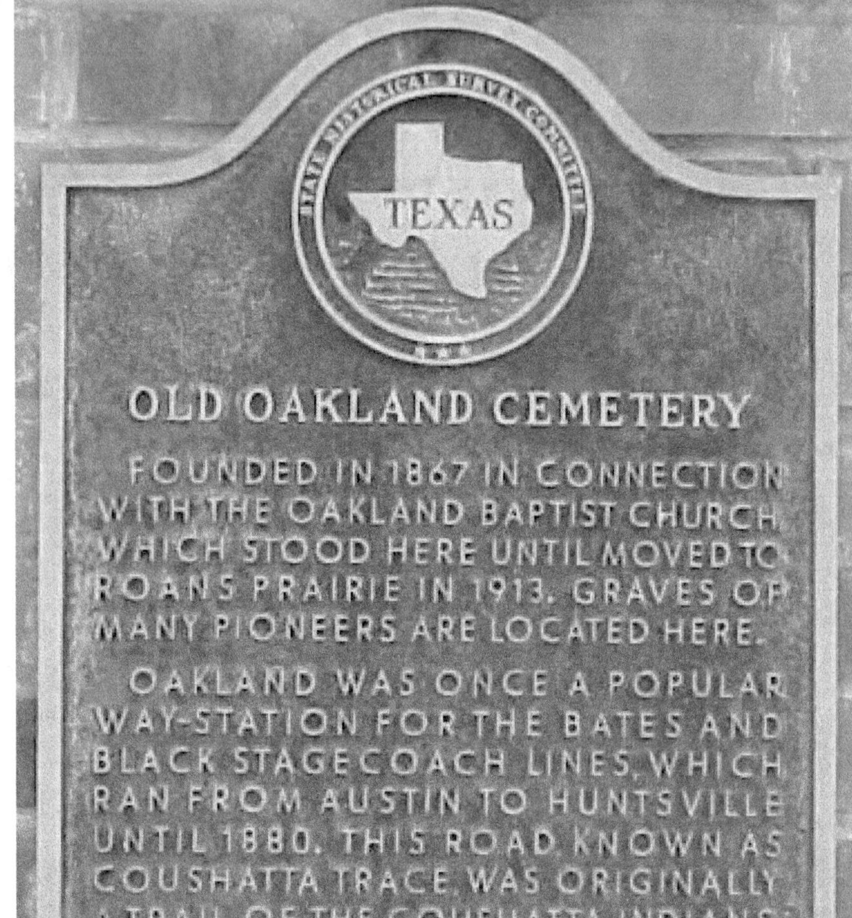


Historical Marker for the Old Oakland Cemetery

# Photographs of the 2004 Church Officers
## Photo's taken in March of 2004

Hon. James P. Dixon
Deacon Chairman

Kenneth Gilbert
Deacon

Joyce Floyd
Secretary

Frieda Floyd
Treasurer

# Pastors of Oakland Baptist Church

George W. Baines
1854-1855

D.B. Morrill
1856-1857

Dr. Justin A. Kimball
1862-1866

James H. Stribling
1869

# Pastors of Oakland Baptist Church

Dr.  James Milton Carroll
1878-1879

G.H.M. Wilson
1881

George N. Cook
1886 / 1912-1913

Joseph E. Boulet
1906-1908

# Pastors of Oakland Baptist Church

W.H. Jones
1916-1920

Tommy McDougald
1959-1965

Gordon Graham
1965-1968

Neal Todd
1973-1979

# Pastors of Oakland Baptist Church

Jack W. Mitchell
1984-1985

Hon. James P. Dixon
Interim Pastor
1994-2003

Dr. Edward R. DeVries
2003-2004

# Photographs of 19th Century Members

Mrs. D.B. Morrill
Wife of
Pastor D.B. Morrill

Ruth Stribling
Daughter of
Pastor James H. Stribling

James Vicarus Floyd

Sarah Parker Floyd

# Famous Texans Mentioned in Chapter 10

Dr. B.H. Carroll

General Sam Houston

Rev. Z. N. Morell

# Photographs from Easter Sunday 1963
### Courtesy of Tommy McDougald

Front (left to right): Don Slayton, Mignon Slayton
(holding baby Todd), Barbara McDougald.

Middle (left to right): Orion McIntyre, Delitha
McIntyre, Lewis Floyd, Bessie Floyd, Bernard Floyd,
Frieda Floyd, Joyce Floyd, J.S. Bracewell.

Rear (left to right):  Virginia Slayton, T.J. Slayton,
Glen Slayton, Ted Slayton, Billy Horn, Ronnie Floyd,
Mrs. J.S. Bracewell.

Pastor Gordon Graham posed for this picture on the occasion of his one-year anniversary of service as the church's pastor in 1966.

# Ordination and Missionary Church Planting

Bill Sandoval and his wife Patti. Oakland ordained Bill in December 2003 to plant a Baptist church in Illinois.

Pastor DeVries preaching the building dedication for Pastor Bill Sandoval and the newly organized House of the Lord Baptist Church in East Moline, Illinois.

# Photographs of Robert E. Lee Sunday
## January 18, 2004

Gene Hightower, Great Grandson of Robert E. Lee, presents a picture of the General reading the Bible to a small boy to Pastor DeVries.

Dan Bates leading the Congregation in the signing of General Lee's favorite hymn - How Firm a Foundation

Pastor Ed – Confederate Chaplain and Circuit Rider

Re-enactors smiling for the camera.

Musket Drill

Soldiers lining up on the Field of Battle

# Photograph of the 2004 REVIVAL

Dr. Roy Branson preaching - February 8, 2004

# Photographs of the May 7, 2004 Southern Minister's Conference

3 Majors and a General Quartet

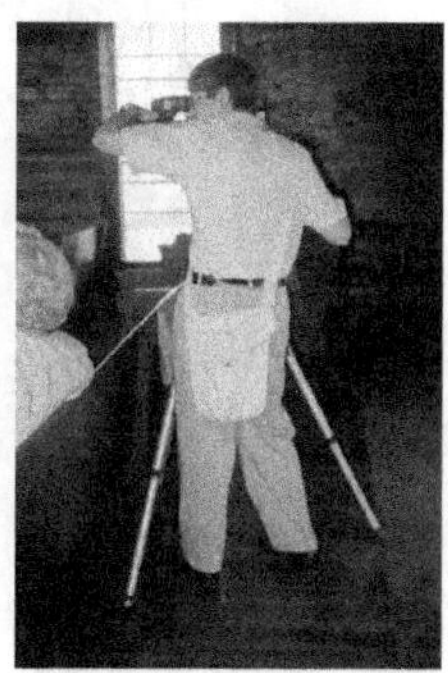

Matt Lee on video camera

# Anderson Baptist Church - Anderson, Texas
Photo taken in April 2002

This building was built in 1853. Oakland began as a
missionary outreach of the Anderson Baptist Church.

Section 3:


# ADVERTISEMENTS
# AND
# NEWSPAPER CLIPPINGS

# Oakland Baptist Church
# Roan's Prairie, Texas

Announces its NEW website:

## www.OaklandBaptist.chweb.org

WRITE IT DOWN!! - CHECK IT OUT!!

Need a Friend to talk to?
OaklandBaptistChurch@juno.com

The above flyer (8.5 X 11) was distributed throughout Grimes County for one month after the release of the church's website. It was also posted on several bulletin boards and in numerous shop windows. Six months later I would still see them posted in various locations.

The above flyer was posted throughout Grimes County and distributed via mass-mailing as an advertisement for Robert E. Lee Sunday.

# ONE-DAY
# REVIVAL

**Oakland Baptist Church**

**Roan's Prairie, Texas**

Featuring Dr. Roy Branson,
author of 14 books, president of Landmark University

# 10 AM
## SUNDAY FEBRUARY 8th

## www.OaklandBaptist.chweb.org

Oakland Baptist Church is located on the corner of State HWY 30 and State HWY 90 in Roan's Prairie, Texas.

For more information E-mail:
OaklandBaptistChurch@juno.com

or call 281-468-3305

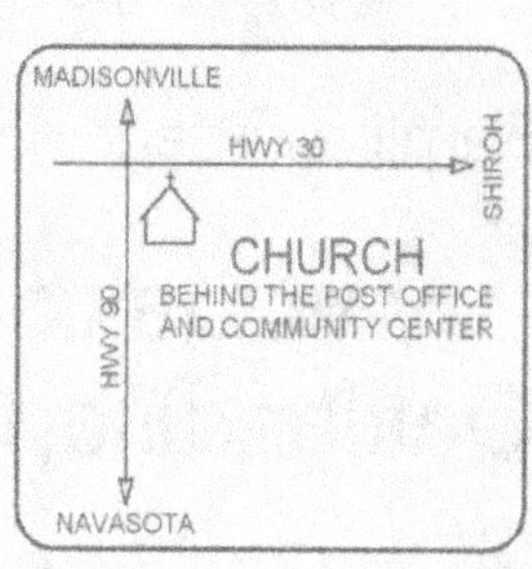


The above flyer was posted throughout Grimes County and mailed to the 74 visitors who attended the Robert E. Lee Sunday. It was also mailed to area churches.

# Easter Sunday Service
# 10 AM
# Oakland Baptist Church
# Roans Prairie, Texas

Special Music by Dan and Linda Bates.

Families attending will receive a free Easter book.

## www.OaklandBaptist.chweb.org
## OaklandBaptistChurch@juno.com

This brochure was distributed throughout Grimes County
during the 2 weeks previous to the 2004 Easter Service.

Creath-Brazos Baptist Association Newsletter
July 1986

Bernard and Frieda Floyd sit in a front pew of their Oakland Baptist Church, located behind the Roans Prairie Community Center. The Floyds are the last remaining members of the church that was organized in 1854.

May 3, 1987 – Navasota Examiner

Headline: 133 year-old Church Down to Last Members

"Bernard and Frieda Floyd sit in a front pew of their Oakland Baptist Church, located behind the Roans Prairie Community Center. The Floyds are the last remaining members of the church that was organized in 1854."

# BENEFIT FISH FRY &
# BAKE SALE

Oakland Baptist Church
Restoration Fund
**Saturday, April 23**
11 to 6
# ROANS PRAIRIE
# COMMUNITY CENTER

Roans Prairie, Texas

(36-2c)

Navasota Examiner ad for Building Restoration – 1988

# The Oakland Baptist Church

of Roans Prairie

*wishes to express their thanks for the contributions. For everyone's efforts to make the bake sale and fish fry a success.*

*Special thanks to the Grimes County Lions Club of Anderson and the Roans Prairie Community Center.*

april 23-1988

*Thanks!*

(38-1c)

## Fish dinners fund preservation of church

ROANS PRAIRIE — The Grimes County Lions Club and the Roans Prairie Community Center will be serving fried fish dinners to help raise preservation funds for the 116-year-old Oakland Baptist Church building beginning at 11 a.m. Saturday at the community center.

The church was established in 1854 on Oakland Hill about a mile from where it is today. The present structure was built of pine wood and joined with square nails and pegs around 1872. It was moved to its present site in 1913.

With money in the church treasury and donations, a new roof and new pillars have been constructed and the floor straightened. The club hopes to raise enough money to paint the building and install new window facings.

# Fish fry set April 23 to help preservation

**By CLARK WHITTEN**

ROANS PRAIRIE — A fish fry to benefit the preservation of one of Grimes County's oldest churches will be held 11 a.m. Saturday, April 23, at the community center.

Members of the Grimes County Lions Club and the Roans Prairie Community Center are sponsoring the meal and cake sale to aid the 116-year-old Oakland Baptist Church building located near the community center.

Although services ended at the church last October due to lack of members, quite a bit of work has already been done to keep the building in good shape, according to Frieda Floyd, whose family was the last who belonged to it.

"I hope that we can open it up again as a church, but if we can't maybe sometime we can have it open (for visitors)," Mrs. Floyd said.

The church was established in 1854 on Oakland Hill about a mile away from where it is today. The present structure, that bears a state historic marker, was built of pine wood and square nails and pegs around 1872. In 1913, the wood-frame structure was moved to its present site.

Using the remaining money in the church treasury and donations, Floyd said they built a new roof, added new pillars and straightened and closed cracks in the wooden floor. "The people have really come forward. We've even had some I didn't even know."

With additional money, they hope to paint the building and install new window facings.

"If we get enough money to do all that then we've preserved the church pretty well," she said.

The Rev. Ed DeVries touches off a cannon shot during a Civil War re-enactment held on the grounds of Oakland Baptist Church in Roans Prairie on Sunday morning. Members of the congregation dressed in 1860s-period clothing to hear historical readings and music during the service before venturing outside to see war re-enactors from the 12th Texas Cavalry and the 11th Texas Infantry put on musket and cannon-firing displays along with other attractions.

Front Page - January 19, 2004 - College Station Eagle

Headline: Back to a different era…

"The Rev. Ed DeVries touches off a canon shot during a Civil War re-enactment held on the grounds of the Oakland Baptist Church in Roans Prairie on Sunday Morning. Members of the congregation dressed in 1860s-period clothing to hear historical readings and music during the service before venturing outside to see war re-enactors from the 12th Texas Cavalry and 11th Texas Infantry put on musket and canon-firing displays along with other attractions."

Section 4:

# APPENDIX
# BIBLIOGRAPHY
# ACKNOWLEDGEMENTS

# Appendix 1:
# Doctrinal Statement
# of the Oakland Baptist Church

1. We believe in the infallible, verbal inspiration of the whole Bible and that the Bible is the all-sufficient rule of faith and practice (Psalm 119:160; 2 Tim. 3:16,17).

2. We believe in the personal triune God: Father, Son, and Holy Spirit, equal in divine perfection (I John 5:7-8).

3. We believe the Genesis account of Creation (Gen. 1; 2).

4. We believe that Satan is a fallen angel, the archenemy of God and man, the unholy god of this world, and that his destiny is the eternal lake of fire (Isa. 14:12-15; Ezek. 28:11-19; Matt. 25:41; 2 Cor. 4:4; Eph.6:10-17; Rev. 20:10).

5. We believe in the virgin birth and sinless humanity of Jesus Christ (Matt. 1:18-20; 2 Cor. 5:21; 1Peter 2:22).

6. We believe in the deity of Jesus Christ (John 10:30; John 1:1, 14; 2Cor. 5:19).

7. We believe the Holy Spirit is the divine Administrator for Jesus Christ in His churches (Luke 24:49; John 14:16, 17; Acts 1:4, 5, 8; Acts 2:1-4).

8. We believe that Man was created in the image of God and lived in innocency until he fell by voluntary transgression from his sinless state, the result being that all

mankind are sinners (Gen. 1:26; Gen. 3:6-24; Rom. 5:12, 19).

9. We believe that the suffering and death of Jesus Christ was substitutionary for all mankind and is efficacious only to those who believe (Isa. 53:6; Heb.2:9; 1 Peter 2:24; 1 Peter 3:18; 2 Peter 3:9; 1John 2:2).

10. We believe in the bodily resurrection and ascension of Christ and the bodily resurrection of His saints (Matthew 28:1-7; Acts 1:9-11; 1 Cor. 15:42-58; 1Thess. 4:13-18).

11. We believe in the premillennial, personal, bodily return of Christ as the crowning event of the Gentile age. This event will include the resurrection of the righteous to eternal heaven, and the Millennium will be followed by the resurrection of the unrighteous unto eternal punishment in the lake of fire and that the righteous shall enter into the New Jerusalem  (John 14:1-6; 1Thess.4:13-18; 2 Thess. 2:8; Rev. 19; Rev. 20:4-6; Rev. 20:11-15; Rev. 21:8).

12. We believe that the depraved sinner is saved wholly by grace through faith in Jesus Christ, and the requisites to regeneration are repentance toward God and faith in the Lord Jesus Christ (Luke 13:3-5; John 3:16-18; Acts 20:21; Rom. 6:23; Eph. 2:8, 9), and that the Holy Spirit convicts sinners, regenerates, seals, secures, and indwells every believer (John 3:6; John 16:8, 9; Rom. 8:9-11; 1 Cor. 6:19, 20; Eph. 4:30; Titus 3:5).

13. We believe all who trust Jesus Christ for salvation are secure in Him and shall not perish (John 3:36; John 5:24;

John 10:27-30; Rom. 8:35-39; Heb. 10:39; 1Peter 1:5).

14. We believe that God deals with believers as His children, that He chastises the disobedient, and that He rewards the obedient (Matt. 16:27; Matt.25:14-23; John 1:12; Heb. 12:5-11; 2 John 8; Rev. 22:12).

15. We believe that the local church is a visible assembly of scripturally baptized believers in covenant relationship to carry out the Commission of the Lord Jesus Christ, and each church is an independent, self-governing body, and no other ecclesiastical body may exercise authority over it. (Matt. 4:18-22; Matt. 16:18; Mark 1:14-20; John 1:35-51; Eph. 3:21).

16. We believe that there are two pictorial ordinances in the Lord's churches: Baptism and the Lord's Supper. Scriptural baptism is the immersion of believers in water, administered by the authority of a New Testament church. The Lord's Supper is a memorial ordinance, picturing His death until He comes again (Matt. 28:19, 20; Acts 8:12, 38; Rom. 6:4; 1 Cor. 5:11-13; 1 Cor. 11:1, 2, 17-20, 26).

17. We believe that there are two divinely appointed offices in a church, pastors and deacons, to be filled by men whose qualifications are set forth in Titus and 1 Timothy.

18. We believe that all associations, fellowships, and committees are, and properly should be, servants of, and under control of the local churches (Matt. 20:25-28).

19. We believe that Jesus Christ alone is the head of the church and that all Christian churches should be free to worship without interference from the government. (Eph. 1:22).

# Appendix 2:
# History of the Town of Roan's Prairie

The town of Roan's Prairie is located at the intersection of State highways 30 and 90, seventeen miles northeast of Navasota in central Grimes County.

The area was first inhabited by the Bedias, Coushattee, Comanche, and Kickapoo Indians. It was in the Roan's Prairie area that the Comanche Indians maintained a lookout point to watch for people entering into their territory.

The area was first settled by white people in 1831 when the Mexican government granted one league of land to Major Joshua Hadley. John Harris was granted one-fourth league of land, and a league of land was also awarded to Anthony Kennard. These three men were all members of Stephen F. Austin's colony of Texas.

Major Hadley built a large two-story house with a nearby fort for protection against the Indians. As a result the area came to be known as "Hadley's Prairie." The Hadley's son Henry was the first white child born in Grimes County.

In 1838, on the site of what is now the Old Oakland Cemetery (it was on this site that Oakland Baptist Church's building sat from 1872 until 1913) a Mrs. Taylor was captured by Indians and cruelly murdered, her children were taken as hostages but were later recaptured. This inspired the first war between the Republic of Texas and the Indians.

In 1841 (1845 according to some accounts) Willis I. Roan moved to the vicinity from Alabama and this is when an actual "town" began to develop.

Roan, with a large contingent of slaves, constructed a substantial log house, opened a general merchandise store, and in 1849 became the settlement's first Postmaster.

It was sometime between 1845 and 1849 that the area came to be known as Roan's Prairie.

A stage route from Huntsville to Austin passed through the town, and a stage depot was erected. An early school, known as the Coon Ridge School, was established north of the settlement. A second school, at Oakland, was established one mile east of town on the lower floor of a two-story frame building (the same building used until 1872 as the meetinghouse for Oakland Baptist). The upper floor also served as a Grange hall during the late 1870s.

In 1903 the International-Great Northern Railroad extended its Madisonville branch line through the community. The Smith Land and Improvement Company developed the site and renamed the town Steadmanville, but the name was soon changed back to Roan's Prairie.

In 1904 a new two-story frame schoolhouse was erected. The I&GN ran a spur to a rock quarry north of town, over which sand, gravel, and rock were hauled for the construction of the Galveston Seawall.

In 1915 the population of Roan's Prairie was an estimated 250. By 1936 it had fallen to an estimated 100, and the town had five businesses. In 1944 the population climbed to an estimated 150 and was reported at that level until 1969, when an estimated population of 56 and two accredited businesses were recorded. In 1990 and again in 2000 the population of Roan's Prairie remained an estimated 56.

# BIBLIOGRAPHY


Published Sources:

Grimes County Historical Commission, History of Grimes County, Land of Heritage and Progress (1982)

Fred I. Massengill, Texas Towns: Origin of Name and Location of Each of the 2,148 Post Offices in Texas (1936)

Mary-Lois Boatman, Revised History of Roan's Prairie (2004)

Joseph E. Boulet, The History of the Baptist Churches in Grimes County: Vol. I – Churches Organized Before the Civil War (1936)

Z. N. Morrell, Flowers and Fruits in the Wilderness (1872)

James Milton Carroll, Texas Baptist Statistics (1895)

James Milton Carroll, A History of Texas Baptists (1923)

Record and Minutes Book of the Oakland Baptist Church – contains entries from 1938 until 2000

Record and Minutes Books of the Annual Meetings of the Grimes County Baptist Association – 1897, 1898, 1899, 1900

Texas Historical and Biographical Magazine (1891)

The New Handbook of Texas (1996)

Jerilynn Armstrong, Texas Baptist Family Album: 1885-1985

Archival Sources:

The Navasota Examiner – newspaper archives

The Texas Collection at Baylor University

The Baptist General Convention of Texas Archives

The Texas Baptist Historical Center – Fort Worth

The Texas Baptist Museum – Independence

Grimes County Chamber of Commerce

Grimes County Historical Commission

# ACKNOWLEDGEMENTS

I would like to thank the following individuals who granted interviews, told their stories about the church, provided photographs, and "fact checked" the manuscript.

Marcus Mallard – Anderson Historical Commission

Mrs. Bill Minsky – Grimes County Historical Commission

Dr. Royce Measures – Historian, Union Baptist Association

Butch Strickland – Pastor, Independence Baptist Church

Dwain Strinkuehler – Pastor, Anderson Baptist Church

Tommy McDougald – former pastor of Oakland

Frieda Floyd – member of Oakland since 1946

Joyce Floyd – member of Oakland since 1959

Kenneth Gilbert – member of Oakland since 1989

Doris Thomas – lifelong resident of Roan's Prairie

Hon. James Dixon – Grimes County Judge

Dr. Michael Toon – Librarian, Baylor University

Mignon Slayton – lifelong resident of Roan's Prairie

Carroll Pickett – Pastor, Shiro Presbyterian Church

Mrs. Gordon Graham – widow of former Oakland pastor

William Borsky – Grimes County Greys

Mary-Lois Thibodaux – The Navasota Examiner

Jack Mitchell – former pastor of Oakland